Fun Fan Facts:
The Unofficial NBA Edition

Milwaukee Bucks

Everything Young Bucks Fans Should Know

By: Jake Liam

How the NBA Works

At first glance, basketball feels simple. Ten players. One ball. Two hoops. Go.

Then the NBA adds the layers.

An 82-game regular season. A draft where bad teams pick first. Playoffs that last two full months. Superstars who can change everything with one trade. Dynasties that rise, fall, and rise again.

And somehow, it all works.

The NBA is built on one big idea: every team gets a chance to reset, reload, and rise again. No relegation. No dropping down to a lower league. Just basketball, every night, from October through June.

It is a league designed for drama, stars, and comebacks. And once you understand the flow, it is impossible to stop watching.

The League Setup

The NBA has 30 teams, spread across the United States and Canada. Those teams are split into two conferences:

- Eastern Conference
- Western Conference

Each conference has three divisions, mostly based on geography. Divisions matter for scheduling, but not as much as they used to.

Every team plays 82 regular season games, usually from October through April. Home games. Road games. Back-to-back nights. Long road trips. The season is a marathon before the sprint even starts.

Win games, and you climb the standings. Lose too many, and the pressure builds fast.

How Games Are Played

An NBA game has four quarters, each lasting 12 minutes. That means 48 minutes of game time, plus timeouts, free throws, and the occasional coach argument that adds another 20 minutes nobody planned for.

Scoring is simple:

- A shot inside the three-point line is worth 2 points
- A shot beyond the arc is worth 3 points
- Free throws are worth 1 point

If the score is tied at the end of regulation, the game goes to overtime, which lasts 5 minutes. Still tied? Another overtime. Keep going until someone wins.

There is a shot clock too. Teams have 24 seconds to take a shot. No standing around. No holding the ball forever. Keep it moving.

The Regular Season Race

The regular season is long for a reason. It tests everything.

Depth. Health. Focus. Patience.

Teams play opponents from both conferences, but they face conference rivals more often. By the end of the season, each conference's top teams have earned their playoff spots the hard way.

The goal is simple: make the playoffs. But there is a twist.

The NBA Cup

In 2023, the NBA added something new to the middle of the season. Something with actual stakes. They called it the In-Season Tournament, now known as the NBA Cup.

It works like this: Every team plays a small group stage during November and December, with special court designs that look like nothing else in basketball. The best teams advance to a knockout round held in Las Vegas.

The winners split a prize pool. Players earn bonus money. And for the first time, a team could lift a trophy before the playoffs even started.

Some fans are still warming up to it. Some players love it. But the moment a team starts treating it seriously and a crowd shows up buzzing in December, it feels like something.

Which, honestly, sounds about right.

The Play-In Tournament

Instead of sending the top eight teams from each conference straight to the playoffs, the NBA added something new. The Play-In Tournament.

Here is how it works:

- Teams ranked 1 through 6 in each conference are safe
- Teams ranked 7 through 10 fight for the final two playoff spots

The 7 and 8 seeds have an advantage. Win once and you are in. Lose and you still get one more shot. The 9 and 10 seeds have to win twice in a row just to earn a first-round matchup.

It turns the end of the season into a sprint. Every game suddenly matters more. Fans love it. Coaches age rapidly.

The NBA Playoffs

Once the playoffs begin, everything tightens.

Sixteen teams enter. Eight from each conference. Every round is a best-of-seven games series. That means the first team to win four games moves on:

- First Round
- Conference Semifinals
- Conference Finals
- NBA Finals

Home-court advantage matters. Crowds get louder. Rotations get shorter. Superstars play heavier minutes. One bad quarter can flip a series. One great performance can define a career.

By the time the NBA Finals arrive in June, only two teams are left. One from the East. One from the West. Four wins away from a championship. Four wins away from history.

The NBA Draft: Hope Begins Here

Here is where the NBA gets clever. Every summer, new players enter the league through the NBA Draft. Teams take turns selecting college players, international stars, and teenagers straight out of high school.

The teams that finished with the worst records get the best odds to pick early through the Draft Lottery. It is not guaranteed, but it gives struggling franchises a real shot at changing their future with one pick.

That means one bad season does not doom you forever. It might actually change everything. Some franchises are rebuilt by a single draft night moment.

Hope shows up wearing a new jersey.

No Relegation. All Pressure.

Unlike many global sports leagues, NBA teams never drop down to a lower league. They always stay in the NBA.

That does not mean there is no pressure.

Fans remember losing seasons. Owners make changes. Coaches get replaced. Players get traded. Every year is a test of direction, patience, and belief.

Stars, Systems, and Showtime

The NBA is famous for its stars. But stars do not win alone.

Teams need chemistry. Coaches need systems. Role players need to deliver on the biggest stages. One injury. One hot streak. One trade deadline deal. Any of it can flip a season.

That balance between individual brilliance and team basketball is what makes the league special.

Fast breaks. Buzzer-beaters. Game 7s. And moments that get replayed forever. That is the NBA.

Once you get the flow, it is pure electricity.

Milwaukee Bucks Facts

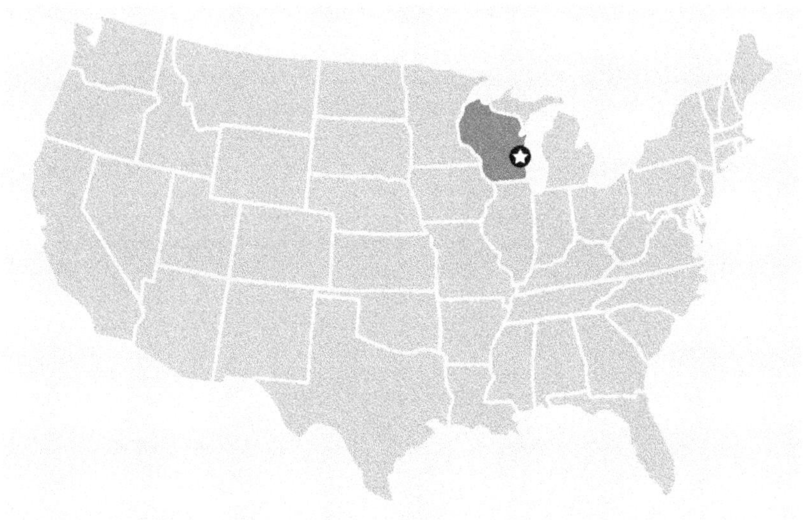

Home City
Milwaukee, Wisconsin

Metro Area Population
About 1.6 Million

Home Arena
Fiserv Forum

Arena Capacity
17,500

Conference / Division
Eastern Conference / Central Division

Famous Local Food
Cheese Curds, Bratwurst, Friday Fish Fry, Butter Burgers

Chapter 1: From Expansion to Empire: The Bucks Story Begins

1. A Brand New Team in a Brand New City

In 1968, the NBA decided to expand. The league was growing, basketball was booming, and a bunch of cities wanted in. Milwaukee was one of them. So was Cincinnati. So was Kansas City. The NBA looked at all the options, crunched the numbers, and decided Milwaukee deserved a shot. Just like that, a city of cheese, brats, and frozen winters was getting a professional basketball team.

Milwaukee was not exactly the first place you would think of when you picture the NBA. It is not New York. It is not Los Angeles. It is a hardworking Midwest city on the western shore of Lake Michigan, where winters are so cold your face hurts just thinking about going outside. But Milwaukee had passionate fans, a solid market, and people who genuinely loved basketball. The NBA saw that. And the NBA said yes.

The new franchise was set to start playing in the 1968-69 season. They had no players, no real identity, and barely a logo. What they did have was a city that was ready to show up. Milwaukee was officially in the NBA. Now they just needed a name, a roster, and ideally at least one win. Two out of three is not bad for a first year.

2. The Name Game

Every new team needs a name. Some franchises hire fancy branding consultants, run focus groups, and spend months on the decision. Milwaukee did something better. They let the fans decide. The team held a public naming contest in 1968 and asked the city to submit ideas. Thousands of entries came in. And some of them were absolutely incredible.

People suggested the Beers. The Badgers. The Ponies. Someone genuinely submitted Skunks, which, to be fair, would have been the most memorable team name in sports history. There was also Robins, which sounds less like a basketball team and more like a nature documentary. The finalists included Bucks, Robins, Skunks, Ponies, and Bouncers. A 14-year-old kid named Ron Longe submitted the winning entry: Bucks. He won 100 dollars and the knowledge that he named an NBA franchise, which is a pretty good Tuesday for a teenager.

Bucks made sense. Wisconsin is known for white-tailed deer. The name felt local, strong, and just tough enough to work on a basketball court. It also aged perfectly, which is more than you can say for the Skunks. Ron Longe did not know it at the time, but he had just named a future championship team. Not bad for a hundred bucks.

3. The Coin Flip That Changed Everything (1969)

Imagine this: it is 1969. You are the general manager of the Milwaukee Bucks. Your team just finished its first NBA season with a record of 27 wins and 55 losses. That is painful. But here is the thing about being bad in the NBA: sometimes losing is actually winning, because it means you get a high draft pick. And the 1969 draft had one player so good that everybody wanted him. His name was Lew Alcindor, a 7-foot-2 giant who had just spent three years making college basketball look embarrassingly simple at UCLA. You might know him better by the name he would later take: Kareem Abdul-Jabbar.

The problem was that the Phoenix Suns also had a terrible record that year. Both teams had a shot at the top pick. So the NBA did what any serious professional sports organization does when making a decision worth millions of dollars: they flipped a coin. Milwaukee called heads. The coin landed heads. And just like that, with the most gloriously low-tech decision in NBA history, the Bucks got the most dominant big man on the planet.

Phoenix lost the flip and instead drafted Neal Walk, who was a perfectly decent player and has spent the last 50 years being introduced at parties as "the guy the Suns got instead of Kareem." That is a tough legacy to carry. For Milwaukee, that coin flip was the moment everything changed. One flip. One lucky call. One dynasty born.

4. The Perfect Pair: Kareem and Oscar (1970-1974)

Lew Alcindor was already extraordinary. In his very first NBA season he averaged over 28 points a game, won Rookie of the Year, and made it clear that the rest of the league had a serious problem. But the Bucks wanted more. They wanted a champion. And to get there, they decided Alcindor needed a partner. Not just any partner. The best point guard alive.

Oscar Robertson did things with a basketball that people in the 1960s genuinely did not have the vocabulary to describe. He was six feet five inches, which for a point guard back then was enormous. He could score from anywhere, rebound like a forward, and pass with a precision that made his teammates look better than they actually were. He was basically a cheat code in human form.

So, in 1970, Milwaukee acquired him from the Cincinnati Royals. Robertson and Alcindor clicked instantly. Robertson ran the offense. Alcindor dominated the paint. The Bucks went from a young team with potential to a genuine championship threat in about five minutes. Milwaukee had found its missing piece. And the rest of the NBA was about to find out exactly what that meant.

5. From Zero to Champions in Three Years

Here is something that almost never happens in professional sports. A brand new team, starting from zero, winning a championship in just their third season of existence. No history, no legacy, no decades of heartbreak to overcome. Just a new franchise, a great coin flip, one legendary trade, and a city ready to explode. That is exactly what the Milwaukee Bucks did in 1971.

The Bucks tore through the regular season and kept rolling in the playoffs. By the time they reached the NBA Finals against the Baltimore Bullets, they were a machine. They swept Baltimore 4-0. Four games. Done. Alcindor, who had quietly converted to Islam and publicly taken the name Kareem Abdul-Jabbar during that same season, was named Finals MVP. He was 24 years old. Oscar Robertson finally had the ring that had escaped him his entire career. Milwaukee had a championship banner before most fans had even learned all the players' names.

To put that three-year turnaround in perspective: the Cleveland Cavaliers waited 46 years for their first title. The Sacramento Kings still have not won one. The Bucks did it in 36 months. Three seasons. That is so fast it is almost rude to every other franchise that has been waiting for decades. Milwaukee did not ease into the NBA. It arrived, looked around, and immediately won everything.

6. Kareem Abdul-Jabbar: The Skyhook King (1969-1975)

When Lew Alcindor arrived in Milwaukee in 1969, he was already the most talked-about basketball player on the planet. Seven feet two inches tall, coordinated like someone half his size, and so skilled that opposing coaches would lie awake at night trying to figure out how to stop him. The answer, most of the time, was that they could not. During his time in Milwaukee he won three MVP awards, made the All-Star team six times, and averaged over 30 points a game in his second season. He was 22 years old. It was not fair. It was not even close to fair.

In 1971, while leading the Bucks to their first championship, Alcindor publicly converted to Islam and changed his name to Kareem Abdul-Jabbar. It was a deeply personal decision that he had been working toward for years, and it said everything about who he was as a person. He was not just a basketball player. He was a thinker, a reader, a man who took his identity seriously. The rest of the world eventually caught up.

The move that made him truly unstoppable was the skyhook. He would catch the ball on the left block, take one step, and release this impossibly high arching shot over his shoulder that nobody on earth could block. He used it for 20 years. Defenders knew it was coming. It did not matter. Trying to stop the skyhook was like trying to catch rain with your hands. You knew exactly what was happening and there was absolutely nothing you could do about it.

Dedication

To every Bucks fan who sat through the cold seasons,
the close calls, and the very real possibility that your
team was almost named the Skunks.

You earned that trophy. All of you.

Fear the Deer.

THE NBA
BY THE NUMBERS

MOST NBA CHAMPIONSHIPS*

CELTICS (18)  †

LAKERS (17)

WARRIORS (7)

BULLS (6)

SPURS (5)

As of the 2024-25 Season. † One Trophy = 4 Championships.

NBA HISTORY SNAPSHOT

1946 — NBA Founded

1954 — Shot Clock Introduced

1979 — 3-Point Line Added

2023 — NBA Cup Introduced

BIG NUMBERS

$156 million
Stephen Curry's est. earnings in the 24-25 season

7'7"
Tallest player in NBA history (Gheorghe Mureșan & Manute Bol)

30 | 4 | 82

30 — Teams Competing in the NBA

4 — Playoff Rounds

82 — Games Per Season

MILWAUKEE BUCKS
IN THE NBA

- **FOUNDED: 1968** †
- **NBA TITLES: 2**
- **CONFERENCE TITLES: 3** *

50
Numbr of Years Between Titles ('71 & '21)

*† Founding dates are complicated & may cause arguments at Thanksgiving. Ask someone born before color TV. All Titles reflect pre-relocation franchise history. * As of 2024-25 Season.*

NBA ALL-TIME MVP LEADERS

KAREEM ABDUL-JABBAR (6) ★ MICHAEL JORDAN (5) ★ BILL RUSSELL (5)

EASTERN CONFERENCE

Atlantic – **Celtics**
Atlantic – **Nets**
Atlantic – **Knicks**
Atlantic – **76ers**
Atlantic – **Raptors**
Central – **Bulls**
Central – **Cavaliers**
Central – **Pistons**
Central – **Pacers**
Central – **Bucks**
Southeast – **Hawks**
Southeast – **Hornets**
Southeast – **Heat**
Southeast – **Magic**
Southeast – **Wizards**

WESTERN CONFERENCE

Pacific – **Lakers**
Pacific – **Clippers**
Pacific – **Warriors**
Pacific – **Suns**
Pacific – **Kings**
Northwest – **Nuggets**
Northwest – **Timberwolves**
Northwest – **Thunder**
Northwest – **Trail Blazers**
Northwest – **Jazz**
Southwest – **Mavericks**
Southwest – **Rockets**
Southwest – **Spurs**
Southwest – **Pelicans**
Southwest – **Grizzlies**

Introduction

Welcome, fans! Whether you're new to cheering for the Milwaukee Bucks or you've been bleeding the team colors your whole life, this book is packed with fun, exciting facts about your favorite team. Get ready to impress your friends and family with everything you know about the Bucks.

Quick Time Out

This book is packed with stats. Like, A LOT of stats. Every fact was checked, double-checked, and triple-checked. But here's the thing about basketball history: not everyone agrees on everything. Ask someone who watched games before color TV and someone who grew up with instant replay and you'll get two completely different answers. My dad, stepdad, uncle, and grandpa all argued about the same fact. Four people. Four answers. All of them think they're right. So if you spot something that doesn't match what you've heard, congratulations. You might be a bigger fan than the people who helped make this book. And honestly? That's pretty cool.

HOW IT WORKS

THE SEASON
82 Games. One Goal.
Each team plays 82 games.
Win enough to make the
Playoffs.
Every game counts!

PLAYOFFS
30 Teams. 16 Make It.
8 per conference make the playoffs.
Win=Advance | Lose=Go Home
Best record
gets home court!

PLAYOFF ROUNDS
Best of 7. Win 4 or Go Home.
4 rounds of pure pressure.
Every series is do-or-die!

OVERTIME?
5 More Minutes.
Keep playing until
someone pulls ahead.
No ties. Ever.

THE FINALS
One Series. One Champion.
Winner lifts the Trophy.
Legend status unlocked.

Wes Unseld of the Washington Bullets battles Kareem Abdul-Jabbar of the Milwaukee Bucks under the basket. Strength meets skyhook as two NBA legends fight for position. *Photo: Wes Unseld and Kareem Abdul-Jabbar. Public*

7. Oscar Robertson: The Point Guard Who Did Everything (1970-1974)

Before Giannis, before Kareem, before any of it, there was Oscar Robertson. In the 1961-62 season, Robertson averaged a triple-double for the entire year. Not one game. Not one week. The whole season. Points, rebounds, and assists all in double figures, every single night, for months. It took Russell Westbrook 55 years to do it again, and the entire sports world lost its mind. Robertson did it first and people basically just shrugged because they had no idea how rare it was what they were watching.

Robertson joined the Bucks in 1970 at age 32, and plenty of people assumed he was done. Those people were spectacularly wrong. Robertson was the engine that made Milwaukee's championship machine run. He kept the offense organized, took pressure off Kareem, and brought a veteran calm to a young team that needed it. When the Bucks won the title in 1971, Robertson finally got the one thing his entire career had been missing. He cried on the court afterward. Nobody laughed. Everybody understood.

8. Sidney Moncrief: The Forgotten Legend (1979-1989)

Here is a name that does not get nearly enough credit: Sidney Moncrief. If you have never heard of him, that is exactly the problem. Moncrief spent a decade in Milwaukee being one of the best two-way players in the entire NBA, and somehow history has mostly moved on without him. That is wrong and it needs to be fixed right now.

Moncrief won the NBA Defensive Player of the Year award in 1983 and 1984, back to back. He was so good on defense that the league literally invented the award partly because of players like him. He could guard anyone on the floor, anticipate passes before they happened, and make life absolutely miserable for opposing scorers. He was also an excellent offensive player, averaging over 20 points a game at his peak, which means he was hurting you on both ends every single night.

Pretend you are an opposing guard in 1984. You have spent all week preparing for this game. You feel ready. Then Sidney Moncrief shows up and spends 40 minutes making you feel like you have never played basketball before in your life. That was what it was like for everyone who had to guard him or be guarded by him.

The Bucks made the playoffs nine straight years during his era. Nine. Without a superstar. Without a coin flip miracle. Just Moncrief, his teammates, and a ridiculous amount of effort.

9. Ray Allen: Mr. Three-Point (1996-2003)

Before Ray Allen became famous for one of the greatest shots in NBA Finals history, before he was a Celtic, before he was a Miami Heat champion, he was a Milwaukee Buck. And he was absolutely lethal. Allen arrived in Milwaukee in 1996 and immediately made everyone forget whoever played shooting guard before him, because Ray Allen shooting a basketball was one of the most beautiful things in sports. His form was so perfect it looked like a geometry lesson.

Allen led the league in three-pointers made during his time in Milwaukee and helped establish that the Bucks could still be relevant in the modern NBA. He was smooth, professional, and almost robotic in his consistency. Other players practiced shooting. Ray Allen practiced shooting the way surgeons practice surgery. He had a routine before every game that was so precise and so detailed that his teammates would just stand and watch it in silence.

He was eventually traded to Seattle in 2003 in a deal that brought Gary Payton and Desmond Mason to Milwaukee, and a whole lot of sad Bucks fans. Allen went on to win two championships with other teams and hit arguably the most important three-pointer in Finals history. He is a Hall of Famer. He was a Buck first. Milwaukee fans have complicated feelings about that and honestly they are entitled to every single one of them.

10. Giannis Antetokounmpo: The Greek Freak (2013-present)

Where do you even start with Giannis Antetokounmpo. The name alone takes most people three attempts to pronounce correctly. The story behind the name is even wilder. Giannis grew up in Athens, Greece, the son of Nigerian immigrants who had moved to Europe looking for a better life. Money was tight. Really tight. As a kid, Giannis and his brothers would sell trinkets and watches on the streets of Athens just to help the family survive. He started playing organized basketball seriously at 13. He was in the NBA at 18.

The Bucks drafted him 15th overall in 2013 and nobody outside of Milwaukee paid much attention. He was a skinny teenager from Greece who had barely played competitive basketball. What the Bucks saw was potential so enormous it was almost impossible to measure. They were right. Giannis grew into a 6-foot-11 point guard with the wingspan of a small aircraft, the speed of someone much shorter, and a work ethic that made his teammates feel guilty about ever taking a day off.

He won back-to-back MVP awards in 2019 and 2020. He led the Bucks to a championship in 2021. He signed a supermax contract extension to stay in Milwaukee when he could have gone anywhere, because he wanted to win it for the city that believed in him first. The kid who was selling watches on the streets of Athens became the best basketball player on the planet. If someone tried to put that in a movie script, people would say it was too unrealistic. It happened anyway.

11. The 1971 Championship Sweep

Most championship runs take time. Teams grind through seven-game series, survive close calls, and limp into the Finals exhausted. The 1971 Milwaukee Bucks did not get that memo. They went through the entire playoffs like a wrecking ball through a paper wall, and when they reached the NBA Finals against the Baltimore Bullets, they did not slow down for a single second.

The sweep was total. Four games. Four wins. The Bullets had good players, a real coach, and a genuine belief they could compete. None of it mattered. Kareem was unstoppable in the post. Oscar Robertson was controlling the game like a conductor with a basketball. The Bucks moved the ball, defended everything, and made the whole thing look almost routine. Finals MVP went to Kareem, who at 24 years old was already playing like a ten-year veteran.

Here is the number that still feels unreal: the Bucks were three years old. Three. The average houseplant has been alive longer than this team was before it won a championship. Expansion franchises are supposed to spend a decade losing before they figure things out. Milwaukee skipped all of that, flipped a coin, made one brilliant trade, and went straight to the top. It remains one of the fastest turnarounds in the history of professional sports.

12. The 1974 Finals Heartbreak

If 1971 was the highest high in early Bucks history, then 1974 was the moment Milwaukee found out what the other side felt like. The Bucks were back in the Finals, this time against the Boston Celtics, and this series was nothing like the sweep three years earlier. This one hurt in a very specific, very personal way that Bucks fans of a certain age still do not love talking about.

The series went seven games. Seven brutal, back-and-forth games against a Celtics team that had Dave Cowens, John Havlicek, and an absolute refusal to go away quietly. Milwaukee had chances. They pushed Boston all the way to a deciding game and then lost it on the road in Boston Garden, where the crowd was so loud the building seemed to physically shake. Kareem had one of the great individual Finals performances in history across that series and still ended up on the losing side.

That was the last time the Bucks reached the Finals for 47 years. One series. One loss. And then nearly five decades of close calls, rebuilds, and what-ifs before Milwaukee got back to that stage. The 1974 Finals did not just sting in the moment. It launched one of the longest championship droughts in franchise history. Boston fans celebrated. Milwaukee fans drove home in silence. Some things stay with you.

13. Giannis' 50-Point Game 6 (2021)

By the time Game 6 of the 2021 NBA Finals arrived, the pressure on Giannis Antetokounmpo was almost impossible to describe. The series was tied 3-2. The Bucks were playing at home. And every basketball analyst on the planet was waiting to see whether Giannis had what it took to close it out. Some people had spent two years suggesting he did not. He was about to make all of them feel very silly.

If you were sitting in Fiserv Forum on July 20, 2021, the place was so loud you could feel it in your chest. Giannis catches the ball on the left side, drives, gets fouled, goes to the line. He does this over and over and over.

Free throw after free throw. Bucket after bucket. By the end of the night he has scored 50 points, grabbed 14 rebounds, and blocked 5 shots in the most important game of his life. The building does not stop screaming for the last six minutes of the game.

Fifty points in a potential championship-clinching game. To find a comparable Finals performance you have to go back to Jerry West in 1969 and Bob Pettit in 1958. The kid who grew up on the streets of Athens put up one of the greatest individual games in Finals history. Nobody was questioning whether he had what it took after that night. Nobody.

14. The 2021 Championship

When the final buzzer sounded on July 20, 2021, the Milwaukee Bucks were NBA champions for the first time in 50 years. Fifty years. That is long enough for an entire generation of fans to grow up, get old, and spend their whole lives waiting for something that finally arrived on a Tuesday night in July. Players piled on top of each other. Giannis dropped to his knees. Head coach Mike Budenholzer pumped his fist so hard he nearly fell over.

The Bucks had beaten the Phoenix Suns 4-2 in one of the best Finals in years. It was not just Giannis. Khris Middleton hit enormous shots when the pressure was highest. Bobby Portis came off the bench and played with so much energy the crowd fed off it like it was oxygen. Jrue Holiday made a play in the final seconds of Game 5 that saved the series and barely got the credit it deserved. This was a team championship in the most genuine sense of the word.

Outside the arena, something incredible was happening. Tens of thousands of people had gathered in the Deer District, the plaza surrounding Fiserv Forum, watching the game on giant screens. When the final buzzer went, the noise that came out of that crowd could probably be heard in Chicago. Cars honked all night. People hugged strangers. Milwaukee, a city that had waited half a century, finally had its moment.

15. The Deer District Explosion

Nobody planned for the Deer District to become one of the most electric sports viewing experiences in America. It started as a simple idea: build a plaza outside the new arena, put up some screens, let fans gather. What happened during the 2021 playoffs was something nobody could have scripted if they tried.

Game by game, the crowds grew. By the time the Bucks reached the Finals, the Deer District was drawing 65,000 people per game into the streets outside Fiserv Forum. People who did not have tickets, people who had never been to a live NBA game, families with little kids, grandparents, everyone. They brought lawn chairs and nachos and painted their faces green and stood in the Wisconsin summer heat screaming at a giant screen together. The whole city turned into one enormous living room.

Sports television networks started sending cameras just to capture what was happening outside the arena. The Deer District became as much a part of the story as the games themselves. When Giannis hit free throws in Game 6, 65,000 people outside held their breath together. When the final buzzer sounded, those same 65,000 people completely lost their minds together.

Milwaukee had not just won a championship. It had reminded the entire country that mid-size cities love their teams just as hard as anywhere else. Maybe harder.

Chapter 4: Bango, Traditions, and the Wildest Bucks Facts

16. Bango the Buck

Every NBA team has a mascot. Most of them wave at kids, take photos at halftime, and maybe fall down on purpose to get a laugh. Bango the Buck is not most mascots. Bango is a seven-foot antlered deer in green shorts who, before home games, climbs to the top of Fiserv Forum and rappels down from the rafters on a rope while the crowd screams. He has been doing this for years. Nobody has ever looked at Bango descending from the ceiling like a heavily antlered action hero and thought it was too much. It is exactly the right amount.

Bango made his debut in 1977 and has been terrorizing opposing mascots and delighting Milwaukee fans ever since. He is consistently ranked among the best mascots in the entire NBA, which is a real ranking that real people put serious effort into, and Bango wins it regularly. He does backflips. He dunks from trampolines. He once rode a motorcycle onto the court. He is completely unhinged and the city of Milwaukee absolutely loves him for it.

The name came from another fan contest, because Milwaukee apparently decided early on that fans should name everything. Someone submitted Bango, it won, and now there is a large deer in athletic wear rappelling from arena ceilings on a regular basis. Wisconsin is just built different.

17. Fear the Deer

It started as a playoff slogan in 2010. The Bucks were a young team, not supposed to do much, and someone needed something to put on a t-shirt. Fear the Deer. Three words. Simple, punchy, and exactly right for a team named after an animal that most people do not find particularly threatening. White-tailed deer are not exactly lions. They are not bears. They are deer. And yet somehow Fear the Deer became one of the most recognized rally cries in NBA playoff history.

The 2010 Bucks upset the top-seeded Atlanta Hawks in the first round of the playoffs, and Fear the Deer went from a slogan to a genuine identity. Fans wore it everywhere. It showed up on signs, on cars, on the sides of buildings. It was the kind of organic thing that marketing teams spend millions of dollars trying to manufacture and almost never actually achieve.

Milwaukee did not manufacture it. It just happened because the moment was right and the words were perfect.

By the time the 2021 championship run arrived, Fear the Deer had taken on a whole new meaning. It was not just a playoff slogan anymore. It was a declaration. A statement about a city and a team that had been underestimated for decades. When Giannis held that trophy up in July 2021, half the crowd was wearing those three words on their chest. Fear the Deer. Turns out the rest of the NBA probably should have.

18. Fiserv Forum: The House That Changed Everything

For years the Bucks played in the Bradley Center, which was a perfectly fine arena that nobody got particularly excited about. It did the job. But by the mid-2010s it was aging, the Bucks were building something special around Giannis, and Milwaukee decided it was time to think bigger. In 2018, Fiserv Forum opened its doors, and the city has not been the same since.

The building itself is genuinely beautiful. It sits right in the heart of Milwaukee, designed to feel open and connected to the city rather than dropped in the middle of a parking lot like an afterthought. The sight lines are excellent, the acoustics make crowd noise sound like it is coming from everywhere at once, and the whole place was built with the idea that going to a Bucks game should feel like an event, not just a transaction.

But the real genius was what they built around it. The Deer District, the plaza outside the arena, turned the surrounding neighborhood into a destination on game nights and beyond. Restaurants, bars, and gathering spaces filled in around the building. On non-game nights people still show up just to be in the area. Milwaukee went from having an aging arena to having a genuine sports and entertainment district, and the whole thing happened in about five years. Not every city gets that right. Milwaukee nailed it.

19. The Rainbow Uniforms and Other Deep-Cut Surprises

Buckle up, because this one gets weird. In the 1970s and 1980s the NBA had a very different relationship with uniform design. Subtlety was not really on the table. Teams were experimenting, colors were loud, and whoever was designing the Bucks uniforms at various points in that era was clearly having the time of their life.

The most legendary chapter in Bucks uniform history is the rainbow look from the late 1970s. The jerseys featured a multicolored arc sweeping across the chest, blending green into red into yellow in a way that looked less like a basketball uniform and more like something a kid designs when they are given unlimited access to a crayon box. At the time people were divided. In hindsight, they are magnificent. They have developed a genuine cult following among NBA uniform historians, which is a real community of people, and they regularly rank among the most iconic alternate uniforms in league history.

The Bucks also spent nearly a decade in a shade of green that looked less like a basketball uniform and more like a rancid avocado your mom spread on your toast for breakfast. Fans were not impressed. The team quietly switched back to a proper, deep green in 2015. And nobody mourned the old one for a single second.

20. Milwaukee's Basketball City

Here is something worth sitting with for a moment. Milwaukee is not New York. It is not Los Angeles. It is not Chicago. The metro area has about 1.6 million people, which in NBA terms makes it one of the smaller markets in the league. By every conventional piece of wisdom about how professional sports work, Milwaukee should be a city that struggles to compete, struggles to attract stars, and struggles to stay relevant. Conventional wisdom has been wrong about Milwaukee repeatedly.

The Bucks have won two championships. They have had two of the greatest players in NBA history on their roster at different points five decades apart. They built a brand new arena that became a model for how mid-size cities can invest in their sports infrastructure and actually get it right. And they have a fan base that, when things get good, creates an atmosphere that gets talked about on national television for weeks.

There is something genuinely special about a city that punches above its weight and knows it. Bucks fans are not casual. They are not there because it is the trendy thing to do. They are there because Milwaukee is a basketball city, has always been a basketball city, and will keep being a basketball city long after anyone who doubted it has moved on. A 14-year-old kid named that team for a hundred dollars in 1968. The city has been proving the choice right ever since.

Chapter 5: The Bucks Today and Tomorrow

21. Damian Lillard Arrives

In the summer of 2023, the NBA world was watching to see where Damian Lillard would land. Lillard had spent eleven seasons in Portland being one of the most electrifying scorers in the league, a player so clutch in big moments that Portland fans started calling his late-game shots "Dame Time" the way other cities name streets after people. He wanted out. He wanted to win. And after months of speculation pointing toward Miami, he ended up in Milwaukee. The basketball internet briefly short-circuited.

The trade cost Milwaukee a significant amount. Jrue Holiday, who had been a defensive cornerstone of the 2021 championship team, was part of the package that went to Portland. It was the kind of deal that makes a front office sweat because you are giving up proven championship pieces for a player you are betting everything on. Dame Lillard at 33 years old alongside Giannis Antetokounmpo is either a brilliant move or an expensive lesson. The jury is still deliberating.

What is not debatable is what Lillard brings on the court. He is one of the greatest pull-up three-point shooters who has ever played the game. He hits shots from distances that make coaches on the other bench physically wince. Pairing that kind of shooting with Giannis driving the paint is the kind of combination that gives opposing defenses nightmares at two in the morning. Milwaukee went all in. When the Bucks go all in, history suggests you should probably pay attention.

22. Khris Middleton: The Unsung Champion

Let the record show, clearly and permanently, that the 2021 Milwaukee Bucks championship does not happen without Khris Middleton. This needs to be stated loudly because Middleton is exactly the kind of player who does everything right and somehow still ends up as a footnote in his own story. He is the basketball equivalent of the person who plans the entire group project, does most of the work, and then watches someone else get the gold star. Except in this case he did get a ring, which is significantly better than a gold star.

Middleton averaged 23 points a game in the 2021 playoffs and hit some of the most important shots of the entire run at moments when the season was genuinely on the line. In Game 5 of the Eastern Conference semifinals against Brooklyn, with the Bucks needing a win to take control of the series, Middleton scored 23 points in the fourth quarter alone. The fourth quarter. One quarter. That is not a misprint.

He has never been the loudest name in the building. He does not have a nickname that fits on a t-shirt as easily as Greek Freak. He is quiet, professional, and so fundamentally sound that watching him play is almost relaxing, which sounds like an insult but is genuinely one of the highest compliments in basketball. Giannis got the MVP trophy. Middleton got the trophy that actually matters. He earned every single ounce of it.

23. Brook Lopez: The Rim Protector Nobody Talks About

Brook Lopez is seven feet tall, can shoot three-pointers, blocks shots at a rate that makes opposing coaches redesign their entire offensive game plan, and in his spare time is a devoted reader of comic books and science fiction novels. He is also one of the most important players in Bucks history and a genuinely underappreciated reason the championship happened. He is essentially a secret weapon who is somehow still a secret despite playing in the NBA Finals on national television.

Lopez anchors the Bucks defense from the middle. When opponents drive toward the basket, Lopez is there, arms up, turning what looks like an easy layup into a very bad decision. He averaged over two blocks per game during Milwaukee's championship run and completely altered the way teams attacked the paint. Offenses that looked unstoppable against everyone else suddenly looked very hesitant when Brook Lopez was standing in the lane looking deeply unbothered.

Did you know Lopez went to Stanford University, which is one of the most academically demanding schools in the country? He is not just a basketball player who reads comics for fun. He is legitimately one of the more interesting people in the entire league. He once showed up to an NBA event dressed as a character from a video game and committed to it completely. A seven-foot Stanford-educated comic book fanatic who can shoot threes and block shots. The NBA contains multitudes. Brook Lopez is most of them in one.

24. Can Giannis Do It Again?

Here is the question that every Bucks fan goes to sleep asking and wakes up thinking about. Giannis Antetokounmpo is 30 years old. He is still the most physically dominant player in the NBA on the nights he decides to be. He has one championship, two MVP awards, and a contract that keeps him in Milwaukee through the foreseeable future. The question is not whether he is great. The question is whether great is going to be enough to get back to the top.

The Eastern Conference is stacked. Boston is good. Cleveland is good. New York is getting good, which feels both exciting and deeply threatening depending on where you live. Getting back to the Finals requires navigating two full rounds against teams that have specifically spent years building rosters designed to deal with exactly what Milwaukee does. None of that is impossible. The Bucks have done harder things. They built a championship team in three years once. They can figure this out.

What makes the Giannis question so compelling is what a second title would mean. One championship can be a great run at the right time. Two championships, in different eras, with different supporting casts, separated by years of fighting through a brutal conference, would cement him as one of the true all-time greats without any asterisks or qualifications. The kid from Athens already has one banner hanging in Milwaukee. The city is quietly, desperately hoping he hangs another one right next to it.

25. The Future of the Bucks

Here is where we land. The Milwaukee Bucks are a franchise that started with a coin flip, named themselves after a deer, won a championship in three years, waited half a century to win another one, and then did it behind a man who used to sell watches on the streets of Greece. If you wrote all of that down and handed it to someone as a movie pitch they would hand it back and tell you to be more realistic.

The path forward is not guaranteed. No path ever is in the NBA. Players get older. Rosters change. The league shifts and adjusts and finds new ways to humble teams that thought they had everything figured out. Milwaukee knows this better than most. They lived through 50 years of knowing it. But they also know something that a lot of franchises do not. They know what winning feels like. They know their city can do it. They know a packed Deer District at midnight sounds like nothing else on earth.

Somewhere in Wisconsin right now there is a kid watching Giannis play, wearing a Fear the Deer shirt, eating cheese curds, learning the names of every player on the roster, and absolutely certain that another championship is coming. That kid is probably right. And if they are wrong this year, they will be back next year, louder than before, because that is what Milwaukee does. It shows up. It always has. It always will. Bango is already up in the rafters waiting to rappel down and celebrate. He has been up there a while. Frankly, someone should probably check on him.

Bonus Trivia Quiz!

You think you are a true Bucks fan? Try this bonus quiz!

1. What year did the Milwaukee Bucks play their first NBA season?

A) 1965

B) 1966

C) 1968

D) 1970

2. How did the Bucks win the right to draft Lew Alcindor in 1969?

A) They had the worst record in the league

B) They won a coin flip against the Phoenix Suns

C) They traded three players to move up in the draft

D) They won a lottery drawing against five other teams

3. Who submitted the winning entry in the contest to name the team the Bucks?

A) A local sports journalist

B) The team's first head coach

C) A 14-year-old kid named Ron Longe

D) The team's first general manager

4. Which of these names was NOT a finalist in Milwaukee's team naming contest?

A) Skunks

B) Robins

C) Ponies

D) Wolves

5. How many years did it take the Bucks to win their first NBA championship after joining the league?

A) Two years

B) Three years

C) Five years

D) Seven years

6. What is the name of Kareem Abdul-Jabbar's signature and nearly unstoppable shot?

A) The fadeaway

B) The skyhook

C) The turnaround jumper

D) The finger roll

7. What extraordinary statistical feat did Oscar Robertson accomplish during the 1961-62 season?

A) He scored 100 points in a single game
B) He averaged 40 points per game for a full season
C) He averaged a triple-double for the entire season
D) He never fouled out in any game that year

8. How many times did Sidney Moncrief win the NBA Defensive Player of the Year award?

A) Once
B) Twice
C) Three times
D) He never won it

9. What did Ray Allen's teammates do when he went through his pre-game shooting routine?

A) They tried to copy it
B) They stood and watched it in silence
C) They timed it with a stopwatch
D) They ignored it completely

10. How did the Bucks win the 1971 NBA Finals against the Baltimore Bullets?

A) They won in seven games

B) They won in six games

C) They swept 4-0

D) They won in five games

11. How many points did Giannis score in Game 6 of the 2021 NBA Finals?

A) 38

B) 42

C) 47

D) 50

12. How long had it been since the Bucks last won a championship before their 2021 title?

A) 30 years

B) 40 years

C) 50 years

D) 60 years

13. What is the name of the outdoor plaza surrounding Fiserv Forum that became famous during the 2021 championship run?

A) Bucks Square

B) The Deer District

C) Fear the Deer Plaza

D) The Green Zone

14. What unusual hobby is Brook Lopez well known for?

A) Collecting vintage cars

B) Playing the piano

C) Reading comic books and science fiction

D) Competitive chess

15. Which team did the Bucks beat in the 2021 NBA Finals to win the championship?

A) Los Angeles Lakers

B) Brooklyn Nets

C) Phoenix Suns

D) Atlanta Hawks

Super Fan Secret Challenge

Only a true Bucks fan will know this.

(No Answer Provided)

Giannis Antetokounmpo made NBA history in the 2021 Finals clincher by becoming the first player ever to record at least 50 points, 10 rebounds, and 5 blocks in a single NBA Finals game. His performance in Game 6 is widely considered one of the greatest individual games in the history of the sport. Who were the only other players to score at least 50 points in a championship-clinching game?

A) Michael Jordan and Shaquille O'Neal

B) Bob Pettit and Jerry West

C) LeBron James and Kobe Bryant

D) Wilt Chamberlain and Kareem Abdul-Jabbar

Answer Key

1. C) 1968

2. B) They won a coin flip against the Phoenix Suns

3. C) A 14-year-old kid named Ron Longe

4. D) Wolves

5. B) Three years

6. B) The skyhook

7. C) He averaged a triple-double for the entire season

8. B) Twice

9. B) They stood and watched it in silence

10. C) They swept 4-0

11. D) 50

12. C) 50 years

13. B) The Deer District

14. C) Reading comic books and science fiction

15. C) Phoenix Suns

NBA PLAYOFF BRACKET

* Fill in your picks and try not to argue with your friends about it!

Part of the Fun Fan Facts: The Unofficial Sports Guide Series

Be the Boss of the Playoffs

You've broken down the matchups. You know which superstar takes over in the fourth quarter. You've seen the bench units that quietly decide series. You've watched the adjustments coaches make when their backs are against the wall.

Now it's time to stop watching and start deciding.

On this page, you are not just a fan. You are the Head Coach drawing up the last play with three seconds left on the clock. You are the GM who built this roster. You are the analyst who saw it all coming.

This is not just filling out a bracket.

This is building your championship run.

Sixteen teams enter the NBA Playoffs. The path is brutal. Best of seven. No shortcuts. No hiding. Every round gets louder, harder, and more personal.

This bracket is your Playoff Control Room.

The Game Plan

1. Survive Round One: Start with the opening round. Which matchup is going seven games? Who has the closer? Who folds under pressure? Make the calls.

2. Feel the Momentum: As you move into the Conference Semifinals and Conference Finals, things change. Role players become heroes. Stars feel the weight. Trust your reads.

3. Own the Finals: Trace your picks all the way to the NBA Finals. When the confetti falls and the trophy is raised, you'll find out who earned it.

House Rules: Circle your boldest upset. That is your official "I knew it" moment.

Choose Your Weapon: Pencil if you want flexibility. Pen if you trust your instincts. Sharpie if you believe in chaos.

Because once the playoffs tip off, there is no rewinding Game 7.

Make your picks. Trust your basketball brain. And let the playoff drama begin.

Fun Facts Wrap-Up

You made it through! You're officially a true superfan!
Now it's time to put your knowledge to the test. Share
these facts with friends and see who really knows their
team best.

Love the series?

Your reviews help other fans discover Fun Fan Facts. If
you enjoyed this book, we'd really appreciate you
sharing your thoughts and leaving a review.

Want more Fun Fan Facts?

Scan the QR code below to visit our site and explore
bonus trivia, challenges, and special extras - including
new teams, future series, and collectible fun as they're
released.

Collect All the Fun Fan Facts Series!

Check off every book you read. See the full set on Amazon. Search "Fun Fan Facts Jake Liam."

World Cup 2026 Edition

☐ Algeria	☐ Scotland	☐ Morocco
☐ France	☐ Brazil	☐ Switzerland
☐ Paraguay	☐ Ivory Coast	☐ Curaçao
☐ Argentina	☐ Senegal	☐ Netherlands
☐ Germany	☐ Canada	☐ Tunisia
☐ Portugal	☐ Japan	☐ Ecuador
☐ Australia	☐ South Africa	☐ New Zealand
☐ Ghana	☐ Cape Verde	☐ United States
☐ Qatar	☐ Jordan	☐ Egypt
☐ Austria	☐ South Korea	☐ Norway
☐ Haiti	☐ Colombia	☐ Uruguay
☐ Saudi Arabia	☐ Mexico	☐ England
☐ Belgium	☐ Spain	☐ Panama
☐ Iran	☐ Croatia	☐ Uzbekistan

World Cup 2026 Group Edition

☐ Group A	☐ Group F	☐ Group K
☐ Group E	☐ Group J	☐ Group D
☐ Group I	☐ Group C	☐ Group H
☐ Group B	☐ Group G	☐ Group L

English Football Edition

☐ Arsenal F.C.

☐ Aston Villa F.C.

☐ Chelsea F.C.

☐ Everton F.C.

☐ Fulham F.C.

☐ Liverpool F.C.

☐ Manchester City

☐ Manchester United

☐ Newcastle United F.C.

☐ Tottenham Hotspur

☐ West Ham United

☐ Wrexham A.F.C.

NBA Edition

☐ Atlanta Hawks

☐ Boston Celtics

☐ Brooklyn Nets

☐ Charlotte Hornets

☐ Chicago Bulls

☐ Cleveland Cavaliers

☐ Dallas Mavericks

☐ Denver Nuggets

☐ Detroit Pistons

☐ Golden State Warriors

☐ Houston Rockets

☐ Indiana Pacers

☐ LA Clippers

☐ Los Angeles Lakers

☐ Memphis Grizzlies

☐ Miami Heat

☐ Milwaukee Bucks

☐ Minnesota Timberwolves

☐ New Orleans Pelicans

☐ New York Knicks

☐ Oklahoma City Thunder

☐ Orlando Magic

☐ Philadelphia 76ers

☐ Phoenix Suns

☐ Portland Trail Blazers

☐ Sacramento Kings

☐ San Antonio Spurs

☐ Toronto Raptors

☐ Utah Jazz

☐ Washington Wizards

About the Author

Jake is a 13-year-old sports fan who loves football, American football, and basketball. He plays soccer as a goalie and dreams of one day playing for West Ham United and helping teach kids to love the game. His passion for sports runs in the family - his dad was a professional baseball player, and his stepdad sparked his love for West Ham. Through the Fun Fan Facts series, he shares the fun and excitement of sports with fans everywhere.